Teach Your Dog

WELSH

D0767427

This looks like a really nice, fun way to start learning Welsh – great book!

DEREK BROCKWAY

Now he disobeys me in two languages.

LUCY GANNON

Anne Cakebread not only has the best name in the Universe, she has also come up with a brilliantly fun book which will help humans and canines learn new languages. I am world renowned for doing the best Welsh accent ever, so it's good to now also be able to speak some actual Welsh too. And more importantly, so can my dog.

RICHARD HERRING

Teach Your Dog

WELSH

Anne Cakebread

First impression 2018

© Anne Cakebread & Y Lolfa Cyf., 2018

Illustrations and design by Anne Cakebread

ISBN: 978-1-912631-02-5

Published and printed in Wales on paper from well-maintained forests by Y Lolfa Cyf., Talybont, Ceredigion SY24 5HE
e-mail ylolfa@ylolfa.com
website www.ylolfa.com
tel 01970 832 304
fax 832 782

"Hello"

"Shwmae"

pron: "Shoe-my"

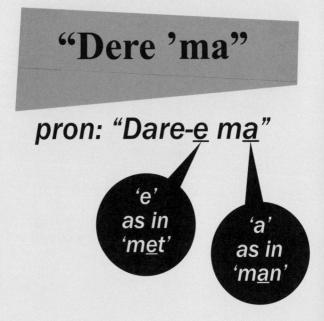

"Don't!"

"Paid!"

pron: "Pied!"

"Do you want a cuddle?"

"Wyt ti mo'yn cwtsh?"

pron: "Ooeet tee moyn c<u>oo</u>tch?"

'oo'
as in
'b<u>oo</u>k'

"Catch!"

"Dala fe!"

pron: "Dal-ah v-ai<u>r</u>!"

silent 'r'

"Fetch!"

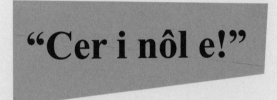
"Cer i nôl e!"

pron: "Care ee nohl e!"

'e' as in 'met'

"Leave it!"

"Gad e!"

pron: "Gaad e!"

'e'
as in
'met'

"Sit!"

"'Stedda!"

pron: "Stair-tha!"

silent
'r'

"No!"

"Na!"

pron: "Nah!"

"Stay!"

"Aros!"

pron: "Are-oss!"

"Bathtime"

"Amser bàth"

pron: "Am-ser b<u>a</u>th"

'a'
as in
'm<u>a</u>n'

"Bedtime"

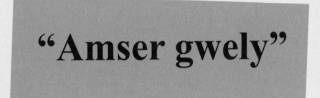

"Amser gwely"

pron:
"Am-ser gwell-ee"

"Are you full?"

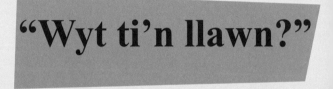

"Wyt ti'n llawn?"

pron: "Ooeet teen
ll-ou-n?"

Put your
tongue on
your gums
behind your
teeth and
blow

'ou'
as in
'loud'

"All gone"

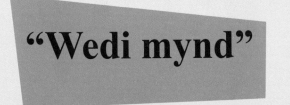

"Wedi mynd"

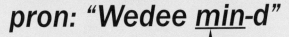

pron: "Wedee <u>min</u>-d"

'min'
as in
'<u>min</u>ute'

"Good morning"

"Bore da"

pron: "Boreh dah"

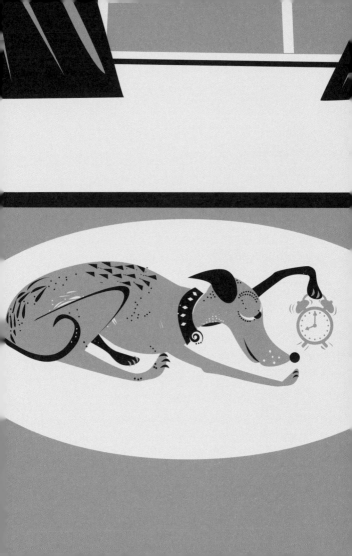

"Goodnight"

"Nos da"

pron: "Nohs dah"

"Let's go..."

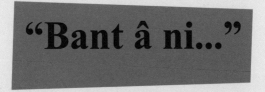

"Bant â ni..."

pron: "Bant ah knee..."

"Go down"

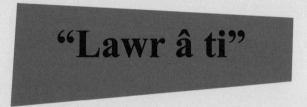

"Lawr â ti"

pron: "Lou-r ah tee"

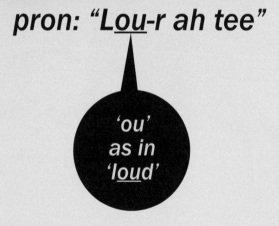

'ou'
as in
'loud'

"Up you go"

"Lan â ti"

pron: "Lan ah tee"

"Go straight ahead"

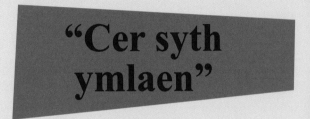
"Cer syth ymlaen"

pron:
"Ceh-rr see<u>th</u> ymline"

'th'
as in
'<u>th</u>in'

"Go left"

"Cer i'r chwith"

pron:
"Ceh-rr ee-r *chweeth*"

'ch' as in 'Lo<u>ch</u> Ness'

'th' as in '<u>th</u>in'

"Go right"

"Cer i'r dde"

pron:
"Ceh-rr ee-r _their_"

'th'
as in
'_thi_s'

silent
'r'

"Turn left"

"Tro i'r chwith"

pron:
"Troh ee-r chweeth"

'ch' as in 'Lo**ch** Ness'

'th' as in '**th**in'

"Turn right"

"Tro
i'r dde"

pron: *"Troh ee-r <u>their</u>"*

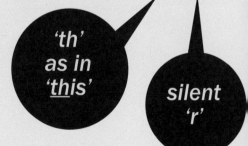

'th'
as in
'<u>th</u>is'

silent
'r'

"Get down!"

"Lawr â ti!"

pron: "_Lou_-r ah tee!"

'Lou'
as in
'_loud_'

"Do you want to play?

"**Wyt ti mo'yn chwarae?**"

pron: "Ooeet tee moyn <u>ch</u>wa-r-eye?"

'ch' as in 'Lo<u>ch</u> Ness'

"Lie down!"

"Gorwedda lawr!"

pron: "Gor-we*th*-ah
lou-r!"

'lou'
as in
'loud'

'th'
as in
'this'

"Say 'please'!"

"Dwed
'os gwelwch
yn dda'!"

pron: "Do-wed 'oss
gwell-oo<u>ch</u> un tha'!"

'ch'
as in
'Lo<u>ch</u>
Ness'

"Can I have...?"

"Ga i...?"

pron: "<u>Ga</u> ee...?"

'Ga'
as in
'g<u>a</u>p'

"Can I have the ball?"

"Ga i'r bêl?"

pron: "<u>Ga</u> ee-r behl?"

'Ga'
as in
'g<u>a</u>p'

"Can I have a cup of tea?"

"Ga i baned o de?"

pron: "Ga ee ban-ed <u>o</u> deh?"

'o'
as in
'g<u>o</u>t'

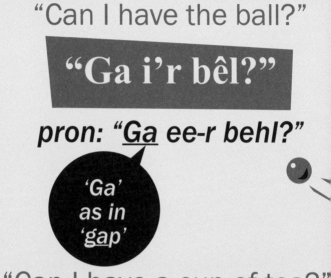

"Very clever"

"Clyfar iawn"

pron: "Cluh-var y<u>ou</u>n"

'ou' as in 'l<u>ou</u>d'

"It's warm"

"Mae'n dwym"

pron: "Mine do-eem"

"It's cold"

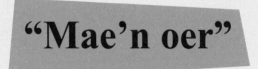

"Mae'n oer"

pron: "Mine oy-rr"

"It's hot"

"Mae'n boeth"

pron: "Mine boy-<u>th</u>"

'th'
as in
'<u>th</u>in'

"It's raining"

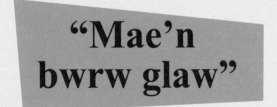

"Mae'n
bwrw glaw"

pron: "Mine boo-roo
gl-_ou_"

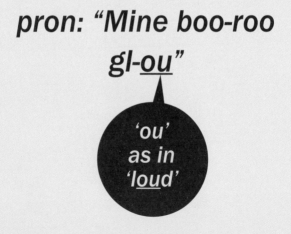

'ou'
as in
'_lou_d'

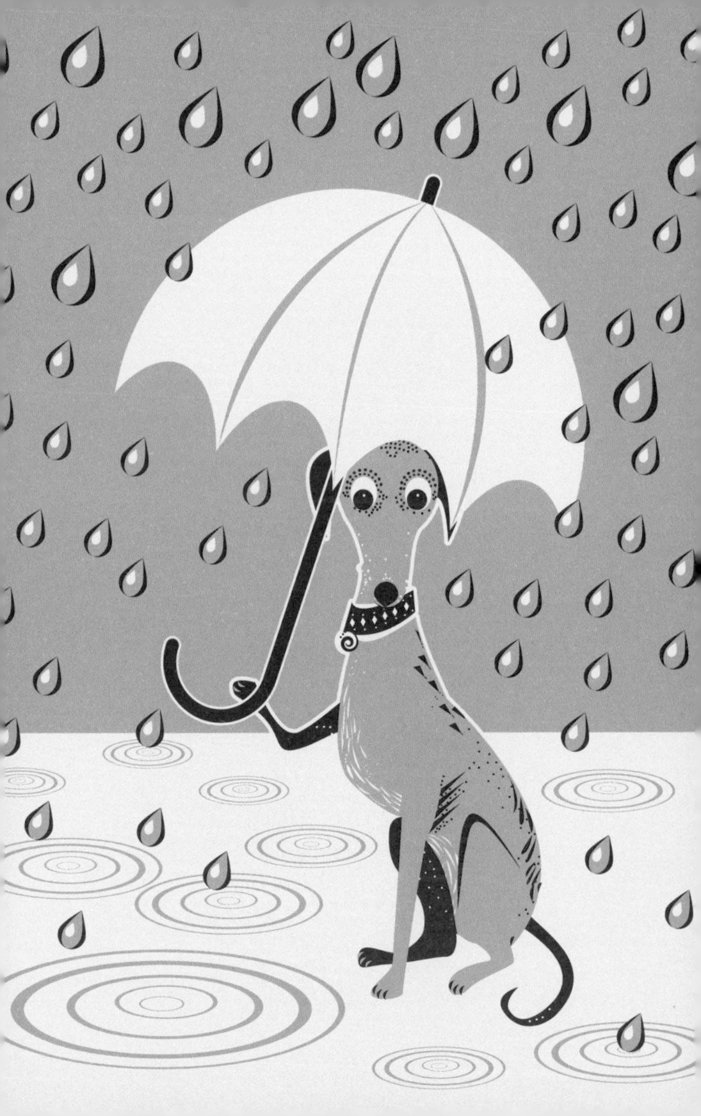

"Are you happy?"

"Wyt ti'n hapus?"

pron: "Ooeet teen hap-iss?"

"Who's snoring?"

"Pwy sy'n chwyrnu?"

pron: "Pooh-ee seen <u>ch</u>wyr-knee?"

'ch'
as in
'Lo<u>ch</u>
Ness'

"Have you got
enough room?"

**"Oes digon o le
gyda ti?"**

*pron: "Oiss digon
o leh guhda tee?"*

"I won't be long"

"Fydda i ddim yn hir"

pron:
"Vu<u>th</u>-ah ee <u>th</u>im un hee-rr"

'th' as in '<u>th</u>is'

'th' as in '<u>th</u>is'

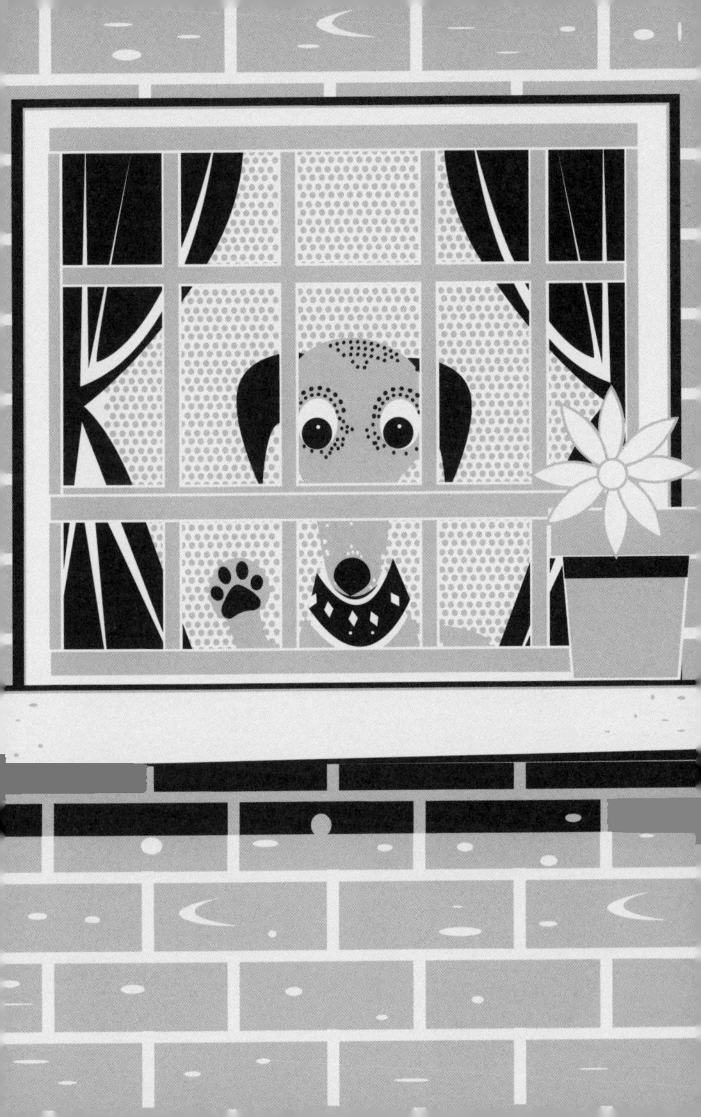

"Be quiet!"

"Bydda'n dawel!"

pron: "Bu*th*an d*owel*!"

'th'
as in
'*th*is'

'owel'
as in
'*t*owel'

"Who did that?"

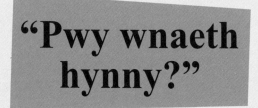

"Pwy wnaeth hynny?"

pron: "Pooh-ee naath honey?"

1 **"un"**
pron: "een"

2 **"dau"**
pron: "dye"

3 **"tri"**
pron: "tree"

4 **"pedwar"**
pron: "ped-wahr"

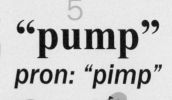

5 "pump"
pron: "pimp"

6 "chwech"
pron: "chwehch"

'ch' as in 'Lo<u>ch</u> Ness'

9

"naw"
pron: "now"

10

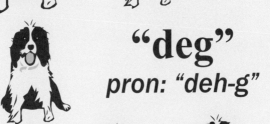

"deg"
pron: "deh-g"

"Thank you"

"Diolch"

*pron: "Dee-ol**ch**"*

'ch' as in 'Lo**ch** Ness'

"Merry Christmas"

"Nadolig Llawen"

pron: "Na-doll-ig
Ll-ou-en"

Put your
tongue on
your gums
behind your
teeth and
blow

'ou'
as in
'loud'

"Congratulations!"

"Llongyfarchiadau!"

pron: "Ll-ong-guh-varch-ee-ad-dye!"

Put your tongue on your gums behind your teeth and blow

'ch' as in 'Loch Ness'

"Happy Birthday"

"Pen-blwydd Hapus"

pron: "Pen bloo-ee<u>th</u> Hap-iss"

'th'
as in
'<u>th</u>is'

"I love you"

"Dwi'n dy garu di"

pron: "Dween duh gary dee"

"Goodbye"

"Hwyl"

pron: "Hoo-eel"

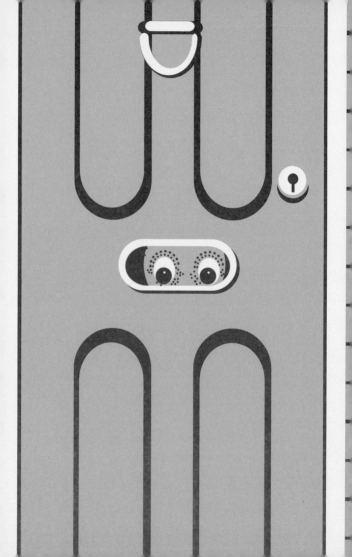

Thank you to:
Helen, Marcie, Frieda and Lily, my family,
friends and neighbours in St Dogmaels for
all their support and encouragement.
Gareth Evans, Richard Vale, Siân Melangell
Dafydd, Carolyn and Meleri at Y Lolfa and
Nia and Sophie at The Coach House for
Welsh translations and pronunciations.
Diolch